A Child's Garden of Grammar

A CHILD'S GARDEN OF GRAMMAR

TOM DISCH

WITH CARTOONS BY DAVE MORICE

University Press of New England

Hanover and London

University Press of New England, Hanover, NH 03755

Printed in the United States of America

5 4 3 2 1

CIP data appear at the end of the book

The poems in this volume originally appeared, sometimes in an earlier version, in *Isaac Asimov's Science Fiction Magazine*.

Contents

A Child's Garden of Grammar

VERBS

NO ACTIVE VERB CAN STAND TO STAND STILL.

IT MUST HAVE ACTION, FEEL THE THRILL

OF USING ALL ITS VERBAL SKILL

TO SINK AND SWIM AND THINK VAST THOUGHTS

AND TIE ITSELF IN TANGLED KNOTS.

Verbs

Supposing a verb Could Verbalize
    The essence of its verbal being,
This Is what a verb Would Do:
                It Would Rise
      Like bread dough full of yeast;
                It Would Fall
Like dew; It Would Sail like the moon
    Across night skies; It Would Call
      Like a loon, and wolves Would Reply.
                It Would Fly,
            It Would Dance,
          It Would Flaunt,
          It Would Frown,
But it *never* Would Think of Becoming a noun.
    It Would Sneer at the thought of Being Pinned down
      Like a man who Has never Left his home town
        To Feel the turbulent ebb and flow
          As cities' millions Come and Go.
No active verb Can Stand to Stand still.
    It Must Have action, Feel the thrill
      Of Using all its verbal skill
To Sink and Swim and Think vast thoughts
    And Tie itself in tangled knots.

ADJECTIVES

Adjectives

Without us apples would be gray,.
And pies would taste like modeling clay;
The nights would go by in a haze,
No darker or brighter than the days.

When we are near, the sky is clear,
The market bullish, stockings sheer.
As jewels on a satin gown
Are adjectives to any noun.

ADVERBS

Adverbs

Gradually they took control.
They would ask each innocent verb
Who came in to the employment office
How she conceived her role
As an employee of Grammar, Inc.

Such questions naturally gave one to think,
Even if one were an adjective,
Living a modestly adjectival life
Out in the suburbs—
To think, that is to say, of what
May actually have been meant by saying
Stop or Go or Do or Dare.

Soon there were adverbs everywhere—
Not just those who'd taken up with verbs
But insidiously clever adverbs
Modifying adjectives!—and even each other!!
The other parts of speech were aghast.
How might they, in plain fairness, resist
These steady adverbial encroachments?
The adjectives suggested, "Let's be more precise."
The verbs agreed: "That would be nice."

And that's how the adverbs were finally,
Though not completely, defeated.

The Present Tense

The future is ahead of me,
    The past is all behind,
But I live in the present, free
    And only party blind.

Epitaph for the Past Tenses

That we once were was all our boast.
The Present came--and burnt our toast.
For us the bidden 'Rest in Peace'
Becomes a jest at our lost lease
On living Life and breathing Breath.
Those who have died must live in Death.

The Future Tense

Someday I will know what to do,
    And then I'll surely act--
Till which time I'll sit and stew,
    A model of poise and tact.

EPITAPH
FOR THE
PAST
TENSES

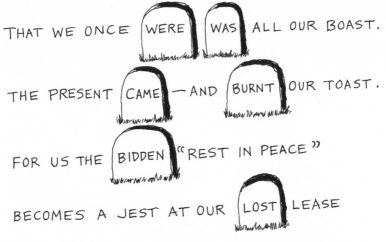

THAT WE ONCE WERE WAS ALL OUR BOAST.

THE PRESENT CAME — AND BURNT OUR TOAST.

FOR US THE BIDDEN "REST IN PEACE"

BECOMES A JEST AT OUR LOST LEASE

ON LIVING LIFE AND BREATHING BREATH.

THOSE WHO HAVE DIED MUST LIVE IN DEATH.

18

THE FUTURE TENSE

SOMEDAY I WILL KNOW WHAT TO DO,
AND THEN I'LL SURELY ACT—
TILL WHICH TIME I'LL SIT AND STEW,
A MODEL OF POISE AND TACT.

EITHER AND OR CAME TO A DOOR.

Either / Or

Either and Or came to a door.
Either would enter, but not before Or,
So still they stand outside that door,
But now their names are Neither and Nor.

IF/THEN

(DETACHABLE TAIL-PAT MECHANISM)

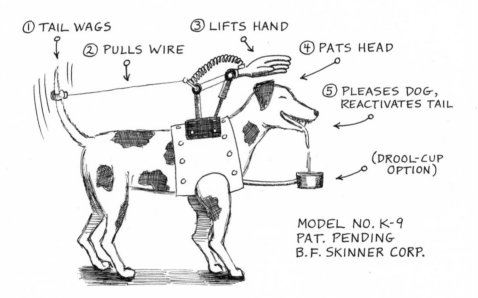

① TAIL WAGS

② PULLS WIRE

③ LIFTS HAND

④ PATS HEAD

⑤ PLEASES DOG, REACTIVATES TAIL

(DROOL-CUP OPTION)

MODEL NO. K-9
PAT. PENDING
B.F. SKINNER CORP.

A WAGGING TAIL WILL EARN A PAT.

If / Then

If/Then is a wonderful machine.
If you use soap, then you'll be clean.
If you do this, I'll give you that.
A wagging tail will earn a pat.

MAYBE

HIS LIFE'S A DIE THAT'S NEVER THROWN,

Maybe

Maybe works another way:
Maybe might come out and play—
But maybe not, he cannot say.

For Maybe's acts are not his own:
His life's a die that's never thrown,
A Phantom jet that's not been flown.

Although he might, he might not, too:
He could be me, he could be you.

NOT, THAT NASTY LITTLE SNOT

Not

Not, that nasty little snot,
    Must always disagree.
If you express the simplest thought,
    He'll say it cannot be.
He'll look you in the eye and say
    Your nose is not your own.
"Good morning," you'll say. "What a very nice day!"
"It's *not*," says he. "Not good at all."
    And if you ask him why,
He'll only turn away and drawl,
    "I can't explain. Good-bye."

YES, IN IS IN, WITHOUT A DOUBT,
AND JUST AS CLEARLY OUT IS OUT.

In and Out

Guess who's the in preposition this year
And who, word has it, is out on her ear?
Yes, In is in, without a doubt,
And just as clearly Out is out.
In is sleekly, chicly thin;
Poor Out is overweight and old.
In has, supple, silken skin;
Out's is afflicted with some kind of mold.
In has dozens of intimate friends,
But Out has only Down.
In has money, and spends and spends
Till envious Out would like to drown
Or seal in a kiln to brown
Or skewer on a javelin
That preppiest of prepositions, In.

PROPER NOUNS

FATHERS, GENERALLY, LIKE CLOWNS,
ARE LOWER-CASED TO INDICATE
THEIR LESSER AND IMPROPER STATE.

Proper Nouns

Some nouns are proper, others plain.
For instance, Massachusetts, Spain,
Consolidated Edison, The Gap,
Our fathers when we call them Pap,
President Lincoln, Senator Dodd,
The Pointer Sisters, Spot, and God
Are classified as proper nouns,
While fathers generally, like clowns,
Are lower-cased to indicate
Their lesser and improper state.

32

THE OBJECT

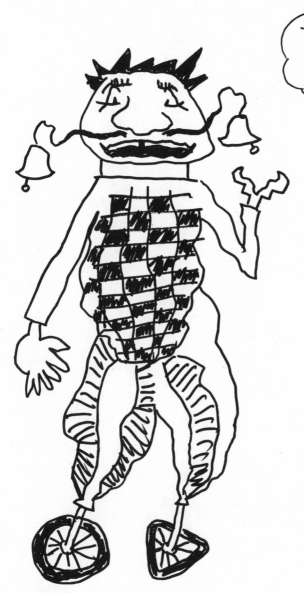

35

THE INDIRECT OBJECT

STARRING "NOOT" THE TALKING TOON PANEL...

38

The Indirect Object

I have to hand it to you, dear:
You're the indirect object here—
Along with Thelma, Hank, and Hugh.
I tip my hat to all of you.
You've set a fine example to me—
But I don't get it, and I'm gloomy.

THE OBJECT OF THE PREPOSITION

The Object of the Preposition

I thought of you and straightway you became
The object of the preposition of.
I thought of her, and it was just the same—
But when I thought of you and me, my love,
The two of us together, I forgot
Every other pronoun I'd been taught,

STRANGE PLURALS

STRANGE PLURALS THERE ARE

THAT LIVE LIKE SWINE

AND HAVE NO TEETH LIKE YOURS AND MINE.

THEIR DIET CONSISTS

OF MILK-FED MICE

THAT HAVE BEEN STUFFED

WITH FLIES

AND LICE.

43

Odious Comparisons

I have been good, but you've been better;
The proof is on your letter sweater.
I'm happy to have been your guest,
But still I wonder: who is best?

You can be bad, but I am worse:
I drink, I smoke, I fight, I curse.
But look at him, whom you loved first,
Who's now so rich, and quite the worst.

46

ATTRACTIVE OPPOSITES

Attractive Opposites

You're beautiful, while I am plain.
I love you quite against my grain.
You're shy, I'm bold; you're young, I'm old;
You're disciplined, I'm uncontrolled.
You're cold, I'm hot; I seek, you're sought;
You're what I lack, I'm what you've got.
You're everything that I am not.

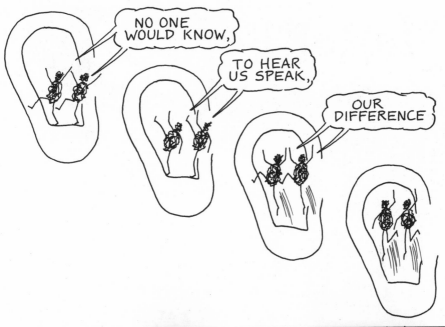

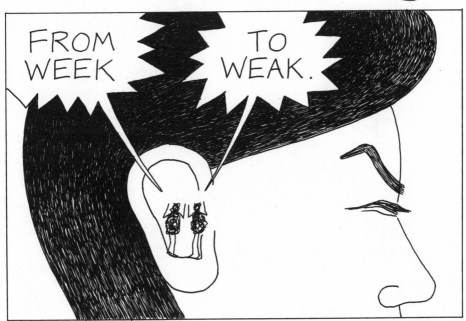

Homonyms

Homonyms

Letter for letter, we're just the same-
And yet we're not the same at all,
For one might be mailed to addressee's name
While the other is nailed to a wall.

LIKE AND AS

Like and As

As I was saying the other day,
Like is like As in a certain way,
And, likewise, necessarily,
I think it is quite plain to see
That As has a likeness to Like,
Much as Pat resembles Mike,
Although *grammatically* they are
Entirely dissimilar,
For Like links things like love and roses,
While the use of As supposes
Two processes have been compared,
Like gardening and having cared
For someone in a nursing home
By reading her some lovely poem
While she nods her head and sews.
So love is *like* a red, red rose,
And *as* the flowers need loving care,
So does the lady in the rocking chair.

LIE AND LAY

LIE, THAT LAZY LITTLE VERB,
PUTS UP A SIGN, <u>DO NOT DISTURB</u>,
WHEN HE IS LYING IN HIS BED,
CURLED UP ASLEEP BENEATH THE SPREAD.

Lie and Lay

Lie, that lazy little verb,
Puts up a sign, *Do Not Disturb*,
When he is lying in his bed,
Curled up asleep beneath the spread.
Then Lay will come along and say
"You shouldn't mope about all day.
Come out, have fun, be transitive!
You've lain about for hours. Live!"

"Enough already of rise and shine,"
Lie would reply as he lay supine.
"Don't lay a guilt trip on me, man.
I lead the kind of life I can.
Is there a law that's been laid down
That says all verbs must have a noun
As object? Or a pronoun? No!
In-transitive's the way to go
For a peaceful sort of soul like me.
Now go away and let me be."

Split Infinitives

To be or to not be's the question for
Infinitives. To speak politely or
To flout the rule that cannot be
Broken with impunity.
Grammar's first law and holy writ:
Infinitives must not be split,
And never ask the reason why.
You may be thinking what if I
Were on a plane about to crash.
Surely it would not be rash
To try to safely parachute.
You would be wrong. The Institute
Of Proper Speech gives not a hoot
Whether you perish or you live—
And won't allow a split infinitive.

QUOTATION MARKS

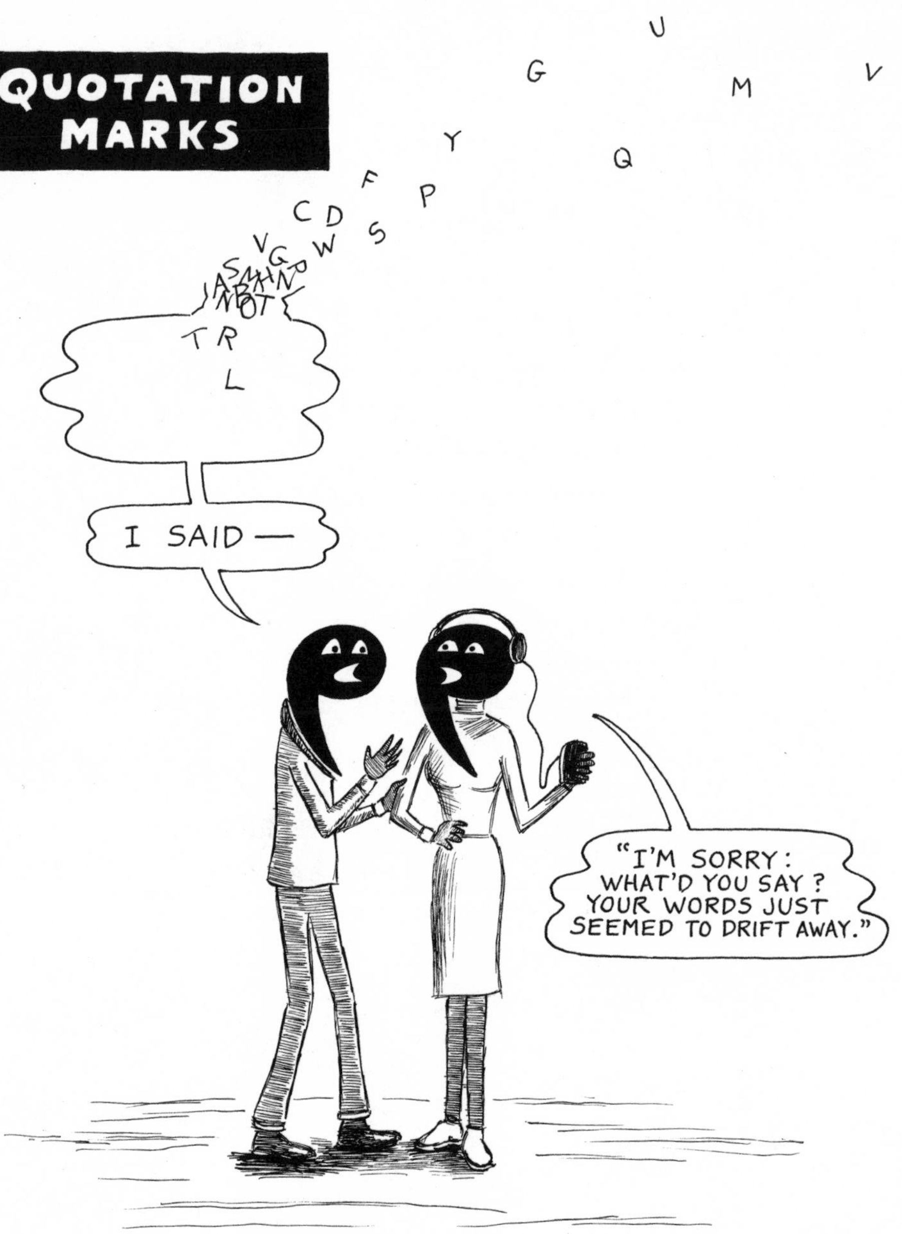

Quotation Marks

I said—
      "I'm sorry: what'd you say?
Your words just seemed to drift away."
I *said*, before you broke me off—
"How's that again? Did you just cough?"
I *said* that when a person speaks—
"All I can hear are squeals and squeaks."
—his speech appears upon the page—
"You'll never make it on the stage."
—inside of squiggles that we call—
"You seem to be behind a wall."
—quotation marks, by which we know—
"Could be your volume's turned too low."
—that someone's *talking*. Would you please—
"At most I hear a kind of breeze."
—take off your Walkman and listen to me?
"Sorry, Mack, but I don't see
A pair of squiggles when you speak.
Must be your batteries are weak."

AUXILIARY VERBS

Compound Object Pronouns

THE GIFT WAS WRAPPED BENEATH THE TREE,
THE CARD INSCRIBED, "FROM JACK AND ME."

Compound Object Pronouns

The gift was wrapped beneath the tree,
The card inscribed, "From Jack and me."

She called him up and asked him why
The card did not say "Jack and I."

"Because all prepositions take
Object pronouns, for heavens sake!"

When, months later, he called back,
She had already married Jack.

THE AGREEMENT OF PREDICATE PRONOUNS

IF YOU WERE ME...

THE LAD BEGAN.

BUT THAT CAN'T BE, MY LITTLE MAN, YOU MUST BE **I** WITH VERBS LIKE WERE.

HE HEAVED A SIGH.

IF I WERE **HER**...

?

THEN YOU'D BE **SHE**.

The Agreement of Predicate Pronouns

"If you were me . . ." the lad began.
"But that can't be, my little man,

You must be I with verbs like were."
He heaved a sigh. "If I were *her* . . ."

"Then you'd be *she*. Let me explain:
The verb to be—" "You're such a pain!

Suppose I said that I were *you*?"
"Then you'd be I, and that would do."

"But you're just who I would not be."
"That may be true, but we'd agree,

And that is what pronouns must do.
You're *not* me. But—I could be you."

You and I

If I were you, who would I be?
Not me, because I would be you.
I'd have your name and wear your clothes,
And if I wrote, I'd write your prose,
Which would not be like me at all.
You want to talk? Give me a call.

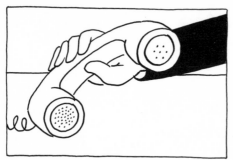

THOU, THEE, AND THINE

THERE WAS A TIME — IT'S LONG GONE NOW—

WHEN THEE WAS YOU,

AND YOU WERE THOU.

Thou, Thee, and Thine

There was a time--it's long gone now-
When thee was you, and you were thou.
I've always been myself, a me,
But how fondly I remember thee!
The whole world now is yours and mine
That once, my love, was ours and thine.

I'VE ALWAYS BEEN MYSELF,

A ME,

BUT HOW FONDLY I REMEMBER THEE!

Definite and Indefinite Articles

Definite and
Indefinite Articles

The, which seems the merest particle,
In point of fact's a definite article-
The word we make more use of every day
Than any article except for *A*.

A's indefinite, as is *An*:
Nouns that have no other plan
For being something other than
A dog or cat, an ape or man
Must take the article they can.

But not *The* teddy bear I love,
For Paddington's a cut above
All other nouns. *A* wouldn't fit
A bear so dear and definite.

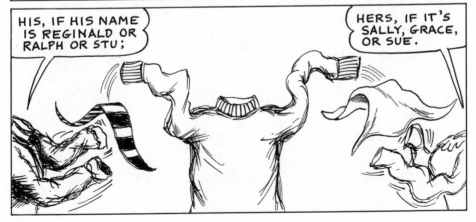

BUT IF NO MORE IS KNOWN OF ONE

OR SOMEONE ELSE THAN WHAT ONE'S DONE,

WE WILL ALWAYS HAVE TO WONDER

WHETHER WE'VE MADE A SOCIAL BLUNDER

WHEN WE ADDRESS THEM AS DEAR SIRS, FOR WE MIGHT FIND OUT THAT THEY ARE HERS.

UNIVERSITY PRESS OF NEW ENGLAND publishes books under its own imprint and is the publisher for Brandeis University Press, Dartmouth College, Middlebury College Press, University of New Hampshire, Tufts University, and Wesleyan University Press

LIBRARY OF CONGRESS CATALOGING-IN-PUBLICATION DATA
Disch, Thomas M.
A child's garden of grammar / Tom Disch ; with cartoons by Dave Morice.
    p.   cm.
    Summary: A collection of poems exploring the world of grammar, covering such topics as nouns, verbs, homophones, and contractions.
    ISBN 0–87451–850–4 (pbk. : alk. paper)
    1. English language—Grammar—Juvenile poetry. 2. Children's poetry, American. [1. English language—Grammar—Poetry. 2. American poetry.]   I. Morice, Dave, 1946–   ill.
II. Title.
PS3554.I8C47   1997
811'.54—DC21
                                                                                  97–23552